Original title:
How to Overthink Life's Meaning

Copyright © 2025 Creative Arts Management OÜ
All rights reserved.

Author: Elias Marchant
ISBN HARDBACK: 978-1-80566-046-0
ISBN PAPERBACK: 978-1-80566-341-6

A Map of Mind's Wanderings

In a field of thoughts, I trip and fall,
Chasing meanings that elude us all.
Should I ponder the stars or my morning toast?
Conundrums abound, I'm the cerebral host.

Questions as endless as socks without mates,
Pondering fruit, is it fate on my plate?
Each nibble's a riddle, it brings such a laugh,
Yet somehow I can't find my other half.

Should I plan my future or just sleep instead?
Overthinking dinners, am I lost in my head?
If I count all my worries, will they shrink and fade?
Or multiply like rabbits on the thoughts I made?

But then I remember the wise old turtle,
He said, "Life's a journey, don't turn life inert."
So I'll dance with my doubts, let my questions twirl,
With laughter and snacks, make my brain a whirl.

Wings of Hesitation

Flapping through thoughts like a butterfly's flight,
Should I chase the daylight or hide from the night?
My mind's a car with no brakes in the rain,
Overthinking my breakfast, oh what a pain!

Is the toast too crispy, or just right in hue?
I'm a chef of confusion in my mental stew.
Each cereal choice feels like a life-altering quest,
Will my milk curdle, or is that just jest?

A parade of possibilities lingers like fog,
Should I walk my dog, or just have a blog?
Perhaps I'll create a 3D model of time,
Or train for a race in the realm of the mime!

Every path I take feels like a game of chess,
With pawns made of worries, they cause such a mess.
In the circus of thinking, I'm the star of the show,
Twirling through questions, as I watch my brain grow.

Echoes of Unanswered Queries

Why is there a sock that disappears,
While my mind churns, riddled with fears?
Is it the dryer or some cosmic jest,
As questions pile up, I fail the test.

What's the secret to finding bliss?
Is it in the cheese or a cat's soft kiss?
I ponder in circles, a merry-go-round,
Laughing at thoughts that have me spellbound.

The Spiral Dance of Doubt

Twirling around in a dance of dismay,
Is this the wrong path? I've lost my way.
The more I think, the less I conclude,
My breakfast cereal feels oddly rude.

Do ducks ponder their pond's grand design?
Or simply quack, enjoying the sunshine?
Is there wisdom in a fuzzy old sock?
I'm stuck in this spiral, just tick-tock.

In Search of Perpetual Answers

Searching for answers under my bed,
Chasing my thoughts like a squirrel ahead.
Is happiness hiding in the fridge's glow?
Or buried in laundry? No one can know.

I ask the mirror for some good advice,
It just reflects back — twice as precise!
With each revelation, I crumble like pie,
In pursuit of the truth, I laugh and cry.

Fragments of a Fleeting Purpose

Collecting my thoughts like stamps in a book,
Each one more puzzling than the last look.
Is there a purpose, or just silly fluff?
Maybe it's just—life is weirdly tough!

I chase after dreams with a butterfly net,
Pondering deeply—I haven't found yet.
With giggles and chuckles, I stumble along,
As chaos and laughter compose my song.

Entangled in Queries

Why does pizza taste like fate?
Is the fridge a portal, or just great?
Why does my sock lose its mate?
Is there a manual for this state?

Cats staring like they know it all,
Is there wisdom in their sprawl?
Do they see ghosts, or just the wall?
In this conundrum, I feel small.

Should I trust my morning coffee?
Or the news, which feels so lofty?
Is my career just a bad hobby?
These thoughts dance like they're all frothy.

Quick, do I need a fortune cookie?
Or perhaps a life coach who's kooky?
I find joy in every quirky,
While my thoughts play like a movie.

A Symphony of Concerns

In the orchestra of my mind,
Each worry plays, perfectly timed.
The clarinet of deadlines, refined,
While the drums of age, keep me blind.

Is my cereal choice just too bland?
Could my plants be making a stand?
Each thought strays like a wayward band,
In the symphony, life is unplanned.

Balloons of nonsense float so high,
Do they burst when I ask why?
Should I just wave them goodbye?
Or invite them for more pie?

With a jest, I sip my tea,
Laughing at thoughts, quite carefree.
What if life's a comedy?
Brimming with nonsense, jubilee!

The Paradox of Being

Why is 'being' so complex?
Like trying to solve a Rubik's perplex.
Do I exist, or just flex?
Dancing in a pool of texts?

Here I stand, a human mess,
Counting my thoughts, can I confess?
Why do I feel the need to impress?
In the paradox, no one's blessed.

Do ducks ponder their own plight?
Or waddling through life, feeling light?
Is silence a sound, or just night?
In this whirl, I take flight.

Who's the captain of this ship?
Is it my brain or just a quip?
On life's journey, should I skip?
With laughter, I'll let it rip!

Through the Fog of Doubt

Am I lost in a maze of haze?
Where questions roam in a daze?
Should I follow where the wind sways?
Or just find comfort in my plays?

Each thought is a foggy cloud,
Yelling answers, feeling proud.
Should I wear my thinking shroud?
In this chaos, laughter is loud.

I ask my plants, "What's the key?"
Do they respond, or just see me?
In the garden of what could be,
Plants and I share a cup of tea.

Through the fog, I trip and sway,
Finding humor in the fray.
Life's a puzzle of disarray,
Yet I grin, come what may!

The Paradox of Seeking Simplicity

In search of truth, I trip and fall,
Tangled thoughts, they bicker and sprawl.
A simple pie or a puzzle grand,
Is freedom hidden in a grain of sand?

I brewed my coffee strong and black,
But why's my mind on a mental track?
To untangle all, I scribble and sigh,
Beneath the stars, I question why.

Beyond the Veil of Existential Fog

Through the haze, I squint and squirm,
Is life a joke or just a term?
The clouds are thick, the punchline's lost,
Yet here I stand, no matter the cost.

With every sip, a new debate,
Is fate a friend, or just our bait?
Peeking through the fog, I laugh out loud,
In this wild quest, I've grown quite proud.

The Unraveling of a Tangled Mind

My thoughts are knots, a great big mess,
Weaving wisdom in daily stress.
A tangled yarn that I can't unwind,
Just what's the point? Am I blind?

I ponder deep, then lose my thread,
As squirrels chuckle, filling me with dread.
But still I ponder, laugh and muse,
Like a riddle wrapped in my own shoes.

Reverberations of Fleeting Certainty

I think I've found my perfect plan,
But then it slips right through my hand.
A certain truth, oh what a tease,
Just like the breeze that shakes the trees.

Joy bubbles up, then twists and bends,
The more I seek, the more it ends.
With every giggle, doubts collide,
Is certainty a joyride or a slide?

A Labyrinth of Thoughts

In the maze of my mind, I roam,
Chasing shadows with a toothpick comb.
Thoughts bounce like rubber balls,
A circus in my head, it enthralls.

I ponder the meaning of socks,
Why one always vanishes, perplexing locks.
Am I missing out on life's grand fun?
Or just overthinking, one by one?

The fridge hums a tuneful song,
What if my leftovers just get along?
Do they plot while I sleep so deep?
In the labyrinth, my mind's a sheep.

But laughter blooms through the tangled haze,
As I puzzle over yesterday's days.
In this quirky maze, I twirl and prance,
Life's a dance—a silly chance.

The Echoes of Excess Reflection

A mirror speaks in riddles, oh dear,
What if I'm just a reflection—life's veneer?
Is my sandwich normal, or does it have flair?
In endless echoes, I find despair.

I wonder if cats dream of being stars,
Or if my car just wants to drive to Mars.
Should I worry if my ice cream dreams melt?
In excess reflection, more questions are felt.

What's the deal with socks and odd shoes?
Each choice feels like I'm picking my blues.
Every small thing grows a crown of dread,
As echoes bounce around in my head.

Yet in these musings, a chuckle breaks through,
Life's just too funny, who knew?
I'll embrace the chaos, let laughter ignite,
As I ponder my sandwich at midnight!

Whispers in the Void

In the void of thought, whispers swirl,
Do ducks ever question the quack of their world?
I sit with my worries, a curious plight,
Jumping from heights that don't seem quite right.

Life's meaning's like a witty refrain,
In circles I trot, like a dog on a chain.
But what if my worries all wore funny hats?
Would they giggle and dance with the whimsical cats?

Ponder all day why I trip on my shoes,
Does fate have a chuckle at my silly dues?
The void whispers secrets, I wish I could hear,
But all I decipher is a sponge's cheer.

Yet in this quest for the cosmic joke,
I find joy in laughter, and hope's gentle poke.
In the void, I'll skip like a stone on a pond,
Life's a riddle; responsibility's a wand!

The Burden of Being

What if I'm just a post-it note,
Stuck on the fridge, lost in the moat?
The burden of being weighs like a stone,
While I fret over snacks I might over-scone.

In thoughts that loop like a rollercoaster ride,
I ponder my queries while snacking on fried.
Is my purpose to find the cheapest pizza?
Or just to ask why zebras are a teaser?

The weight of existence is hard to ignore,
Yet I try to embrace it and ask for more.
With a chuckle that bubbles from deep down inside,
I'll wear my confusion as a clown with pride.

So here's to the weight that keeps us awake,
To the laughter and love, and the silly mistakes.
Life's a zany circus, so come take a seat,
Let's dance with the burdens and stay on our feet!

The Paralyzing Power of Possibility

In a world where choices bloom,
Like flowers in every room,
Each petal whispers, "Pick me, roam!"
Yet here I sit, lost at home.

Should I take the left or right?
The thought alone gives me a fright!
With too many paths to choose,
I find myself more likely to snooze.

A gourmet meal or a snack?
But what if I don't bounce back?
Each bite could lead to great delight,
Or so I think, then lose my sight.

In endless loops, my thoughts do race,
Yet I can't seem to find my place.
I'll stick with options one or two,
And maybe try the sky for blue.

Fleeting Moments of Understanding

Once I grasped the essence clear,
Like jelly slipping from my sphere.
A moment bright, then gone from view,
It's like a sneeze that starts to brew.

Why does wisdom feel so bright,
Yet slip away by morning light?
I nod along, pretend I know,
Then lose the thread—it steals my flow.

Philosophy, you tricky beast,
You never let my brain find peace.
I chase the thoughts like kids at play,
But they just giggle and run away!

I write my thoughts on napkin scraps,
In hopes to catch those silly traps.
When all I wanted was a thought,
Yet here I am, with more than I sought.

The Nest of Self-Doubt

In a cozy nook, I sit and stew,
With doubts like birds, they chirp anew.
"Am I enough? Should I take flight?"
While squirrels laugh from branches high.

Each crumb of confidence I find,
Is tossed aside by worry's grind.
"Should I eat the cake or skip the slice?"
How can such choices feel precise?

In my heart nests a little fear,
Like a squirrel hoarding snacks to steer.
Yet sometimes, I take off my shield,
And ponder what my heart might yield.

So here I sit, with doubts in tow,
Wondering if I'll ever know.
The courage grows like vines entwined,
But then I trip—oh, never mind!

Fragments of Fragmentation

My thoughts are like a puzzle, torn,
With edges swirling, slightly worn.
I glue them down, yet they won't stick,
The more I try, the more they flick.

Ideas scatter like confetti,
Stuck to walls, they feel so petty.
What was the point? I can't recall,
Each flashing thought, a tiny sprawl.

In the chaos, sanity hides,
But sometimes laughs as doubt abides.
"Just let it go! Embrace the mess!"
I answer back—oh, what a stress!

So here I am, a jigsaw piece,
Trying to find my way to peace.
With fragments dancing in my brain,
Artistry in silly strain.

In Search of Solace and Reason

I ponder every choice I make,
From morning coffee to birthday cake.
Is it fate or just my mind?
Oh, what a funny mess I find.

The socks I wear, mismatched and wild,
Do they speak of wisdom or just a child?
If I step left or right in line,
Will the universe send me a sign?

Each laugh I share, a careful plot,
Is it joy, or just a trivial thought?
I chase the meaning in the breeze,
Like squirrels on trees, acting with ease.

At night I lie, my brain on spin,
Counting thoughts as they crawl in.
The quest for sense feels like a joke,
Who knew wisdom's path was made of smoke?

The Tangle of Considered Choices

Should I eat the cake or just a slice?
Every crumb feels like a grand device.
With frosting swirls and chocolate dreams,
Am I wise, or caught in schemes?

Should I call my friend or let it wait?
Does texting first seal my fate?
Staring at my phone's bright glow,
Is this wisdom, or just low?

Each Netflix show demands a choice,
Do I binge or heed the voice?
The plot's absurdity makes me grin,
A reflection of where I've been!

Decisions, decisions, they swirl like soup,
Life's a circus, and I'm the loop.
In every choice, a hint of jest,
Perhaps absurdity's truly best?

Reflections on a Fleeting Existence

In mirrors, faces twist and twine,
What a spectacle to define!
Do I laugh, or shed a tear?
Existence feels like a wild frontier.

I glance at clocks, they tick and hum,
Is time a friend, or just a drum?
I ponder yesterdays with flair,
Lost in moments, I gasp for air.

With each sunrise, I grab a thought,
Is there meaning, or just what I sought?
The sun shines bright, the day a gift,
Yet silly worries give me a lift.

Then I smile at clouds up high,
Maybe I'm just here to fly.
In fleeting moments, I find delight,
And ponder life under its light.

The Riddle of Inner Dialogue

I sit and chat with thoughts in my head,
Is that normal? I wonder in dread.
Arguments spark like popcorn in a pan,
Am I losing it, or just a fan?

Who's that voice, so witty and bright?
Is it wisdom or a clever fright?
My inner self, a curious chap,
Often gives me a mindless clap.

Should I dive deep, or stay up high?
Each twist and turn makes me sigh.
In riddles wrapped like a cozy blanket,
Overthinking feels like a wild pranket.

Yet laughter spills as I untangle,
Life's a riddle, a friendly jangle.
With each thought, a giggle appears,
Perhaps I'll dance through all my fears!

Shadows of Meaning in Silent Moments

Late at night, the tick of the clock,
Thoughts whirl like a frenzied sock.
Do raindrops know what they're about?
One splashes down, while others flout.

My cat stares hard at the wall,
Does she ponder? Or just enthrall?
Is she a guru in disguise?
With wisdom passing through her eyes?

Echoes of laughter fill the air,
Do they mean something? Do I care?
A bread crumb trail of sheer delight,
Leading me to existential fright.

A pickle jar with too many thoughts,
Is too much brine a thing that rots?
I ponder deep beneath the beams,
While chasing down my wildest dreams.

The Puzzle of Our Many Selves.

Am I the me in the mirror's glare?
Or just a thought that hangs in air?
As I juggle masks, who's wearing whom?
Is this the stage or just the room?

I'm bold and brave in front of a crowd,
Yet trip on clouds when I'm feeling loud.
Do I compose my own grand play?
Or just improvise, come what may?

The inner critic's got a loud voice,
In a world of options, I lose my choice.
Should I be serious, or wear a hat?
A clown today, tomorrow a diplomat?

With every laugh, a truth could surface,
Am I just quirky, or do I have purpose?
Let's dive into the fun with zest,
In this silly game, I'll beat the rest.

The Weight of Questions Unspoken

Why does cheese always taste so good?
Is it profound? Or misunderstood?
The weight of questions hang like mist,
And yet, I bounce, I laugh, I twist.

Should I choose between cake and pie?
Is that the secret to getting by?
A slice of life, a nibble of fun,
In this great quest, I'm never done.

If ducklings know more than I,
Should I quit pondering and just fly?
They quack and waddle without a care,
While I sit here, ruminating bare.

Over tea with biscuits, I debate,
Does meaning come from fate or plate?
I'll wait for answers with a grin,
Sipping slowly, letting life begin.

Threads of Infinite Possibility

Spaghetti dreams twirl in my mind,
Each strand a thought, uniquely entwined.
If I pull one, does the sauce spill?
Or does it summon an odd thrill?

The future's a yarn ball I can't unwind,
With knots of regret and joy combined.
As I knit together my daily quest,
Will I end up cozy? Or lost in the mess?

An octopus juggles truths unknown,
While I struggle to find my tone.
Can laughter be the key to the door?
Or is that just a funny folklore?

In the loom of life, I dance and weave,
Searching for threads I can believe.
Is meaning found in the wacky, the weird?
Or just in moments deeply steered?

The Maze of Unanswered Questions

In the maze of my own head,
I ponder what I said.
Did I leave the stove on?
Or is that my pet's con?

Chasing squirrels of thought,
In knots, I'm often caught.
Is it deep or just vague?
Oh wait, there's a new plague!

Maps leading nowhere fast,
I'm lost in shadows cast.
What should be simple joys,
Turn into whispering noise.

Replaying every scene,
Where have I been? What's gleaned?
A laugh in the confusion,
Life's just a wild illusion.

Reflection Pools of the Soul

I gaze into my pool,
And see my inner fool.
With rubber ducks for thought,
A jester, that's all I've got.

Reflections swim and sway,
Do I dance? Or decay?
With every splash I make,
I wonder what's at stake.

The water ripples and bends,
Making sense, it contends.
But all I hear is quack,
Am I on the right track?

Pooling doubts, a grand show,
Who knew thoughts could overflow?
Grinning at my splashed fears,
I drown them all in cheers.

The Dance of Complexity and Simplicity

Step one, I twirl around,
In chaos I am unbound.
Step two, it's all too clear,
Simplicity is what I fear.

Waltzing through my tangled mind,
Finding joy in the blind.
Trip on thoughts, I laugh out loud,
Who knew pondering could draw a crowd?

Jive with questions, twist with doubt,
Do I stand tall or just pout?
In the dance of wits and whim,
I shimmy to the edge of dim.

With every misstep, life's a game,
Complexity is just so lame.
So here I am, twirling away,
Laughing through every dismay.

Timid Steps Through the Mind's Garden

In the garden of my brain,
I tiptoe, feel the strain.
Why are daisies so bold?
And do dreams ever get old?

Petals fall like worries,
In thoughts, I hurry in flurries.
Should I water or just wait?
Every choice feels like fate.

Bumblebees of doubt buzz round,
In this maze, I've firmly found.
Is that a weed or a friend?
Will the madness ever end?

But I smile at the mess,
Who knew worry could impress?
Though timid, I have my say,
In the garden, I'll stay and play.

As the Mind Wanders

Thoughts bounce like rubber balls,
Chasing shadows down the halls.
Is a donut round? Is it a ring?
Ah, but listen to the wisdom it can bring!

The fridge hums like a wise old sage,
While I ponder life from my mental cage.
If I'm just a blip, what's the point of snacks?
Now my stomach growls, while my mind relax.

Do chairs have feelings, stuck in a row?
What's the secret they'll never show?
With every sip of my lukewarm tea,
I ponder deep thoughts that escape with glee.

In a whirlwind of laughter, I spin and twirl,
Life's grand questions make my head whirl.
But at the end of this mental spree,
I'll settle for pizza—just let it be!

Charting the Undefined Path

Mapping my thoughts like a messy kite,
Do stars even care if they shine at night?
I scribble theories on a napkin's face,
While contemplating the meaning of space.

Do socks have a secret life in a dryer?
Do they plot against our socks, ever higher?
With every tumble, do they hoop and cheer?
Or do they craft their escape plan in fear?

Count all the wrinkles on my forehead creased,
Each crease a puzzle, but I'm not released.
Is it age or wisdom, what's that allure?
Or just the result of last night's detour?

In this journey of giggles and mind's quirk,
I'll let my thoughts play, that's my hard work.
If life's big meaning is lost in this chart,
I'll tickle the muse until it departs!

A Mosaic of Fleeting Thoughts

Thoughts flit and flutter like butterflies bright,
Each one's a riddle, gives me a bite.
Is it all grand, or just a bad joke?
With sanity cracked, I smile and poke.

My mind's a jigsaw, pieces all tossed,
Searching for meaning? Oh, how I'm lost!
Maybe it's pizza or a game of chess,
Could life just be a never-ending mess?

Should I really ponder the cosmos tonight?
Or dive into Netflix, get cozy, hold tight.
Why chase wordy ghosts, it sounds a bit rough,
When I have fried noodles just waiting for stuff?

In a collage of giggles and puzzled delight,
I frame every chaos, embrace the flight.
For in the mosaic of laughter and cheers,
Maybe that's meaning, beyond all my fears!

The Tangle of Time and Thought

Time ticks and tocks, a mischievous thief,
Stealing away precious moments of grief.
Did I leave the oven on? Is my toast burnt?
Oh wait, what was I doing? My mind's quite pervert!

Questions unravel like yarns in a ball,
Why does the cat prefer the box over all?
Is that the meaning? Or just pure fluff?
For answers I seek are a bit too tough!

In the circus of thought, I juggle and mime,
Silly like clowns, I dance through the grime.
With every crazy turn, I can't hide my cheer,
Life's just a giggle—come laugh with no fear!

As time twirls around, I give it a whirl,
My tangled thoughts sashay, they twirl and they swirl.
So here's to the crazy, the laughter, the plot—
The meaning of life? Let's just be a lot!

The Fog of Mixed Reflections

In the mirror, I see two,
One's smiling, the other's blue.
Do they argue or agree?
Oh, this is quite a sight to see!

Breakfast thoughts while pouring tea,
Am I human, or just a bee?
Buzzing here, buzzing there,
What's the point? Do I even care?

Dreams that dance like silly clowns,
Chasing whims through sleepy towns.
Is a turtle a wise old sage?
Or just stuck in its own cage?

Questions spiral, like a kite,
Tangled up in morning light.
I'll just laugh and let it be,
Whatever happens, happens to me!

Musings on the Edge of Reason

Balancing thoughts on a tightrope high,
With reasons waving, oh my, oh my!
Should I leap, or stay right here?
What if my lunch is waiting near?

The cat thinks it knows all the plans,
It sits and stares as time expands.
Is it watching or just dreaming?
Maybe it's the cat that's scheming?

Chasing shadows of what could be,
Frogs in suits, sipping sweet tea.
While pondering if fish can fly,
I guess I'll just take a nap and sigh.

A fish in shoes would sure be odd,
Does it run or just applaud?
With every thought, the giggles grow,
In this madness, there's more to sow!

Intersections of Reality and Reverie

In a world where socks are lost,
Are they heroes? What's the cost?
Each dryer spins a tale so grand,
Gremlins dance with rubber bands.

Butterflies wear tiny crowns,
While walking through my kitchen downs.
They flap around like royalty,
Is it madness or clarity?

Pizza debates with a carrot stick,
Who will win? Is it a trick?
While they squabble, I just munch,
Taking life easy with a crunch.

Dreams collide in silly ways,
Stars gossip in a cosmic gaze.
With laughter ringing in my head,
I embrace the chaos instead!

The Stillness of Unending Queries

In the garden, weeds just laugh,
They think they're wiser than the path.
While daisies nod and shake their heads,
I wonder if they fear our dread.

Pondering if clouds wear shoes,
Or just float, with nothing to lose.
Should I chase them with a net?
Or just sit and send a text?

Hot dogs ponder their fate on plates,
While mustard debates with the fate of mates.
Are we all just toppings, you see?
Seeking the hotdog of life's spree?

The sun might giggle, the moon may sigh,
As twinkling stars make a wink or cry.
In the quiet, chaos has a say,
Shuffling questions, come what may!

The Unraveling of Certainty

Why chase the answers in a spiral dance?
I trip on my thoughts, can't catch a glance.
Like socks in the dryer, they vanish with glee,
Left wondering if it's just me or the spree.

I ponder the pizza, with toppings so bright,
While counting the stars, is that really right?
The wish upon one might lead to a fall,
Should I grab a snack or just ponder it all?

Chasing my tail, I try to be wise,
Each question a riddle in a fun disguise.
A parade of thoughts, they march all around,
As I stand in a circle, confusion profound.

But isn't it quirky, this tangled embrace?
Life's just a puzzle, a slapstick race.
With laughter the key, and chaos our song,
We'll dance through the questions, it won't take long.

Footprints in the Sands of Uncertainty

Each step in the sand feels slightly askew,
With questions that bubble like morning dew.
I wonder what answers the ocean might sing,
But all that I hear is the gull's silly wing.

I've lost all my maps in a sandstorm spree,
My compass is laughing, 'Just follow me!'
The tide rolls in, pokes fun at my plight,
As I giggle and stumble into the night.

The footprints I leave might wash right away,
But can't I just joke? It's a brand new day!
What fate befalls those who fret and who frown?
Perhaps I'll just sit and watch waves roll down.

Oh, footprints, dear footprints, where do you lead?
To questions of grandeur, or maybe just greed?
I'll play in the surf, let the water be free,
And dance with the drama, not bound by decree.

Pages in the Book of What-Ifs

In the library of questions, I trip on a cue,
Each chapter a riddle, where am I? Who knew?
What if I'm lost, but not really that stuck?
I'll chuckle at fate, it's all just good luck!

Oh, what if the dog talked and shared all he knows?
Or what if a tree became my new prose?
Each page turns softly, whispers of doubt,
As I flip through the stories, no end in sight, out.

A plot twist appears, my pencil does reel,
With absurdities sprouting, it feels rather real.
Like popcorn machines that never do pop,
The pages keep turning, I just can't stop!

So, here's to the what-ifs, the giggles they bring,
In a world full of puzzles, we learn how to sing.
With laughter as ink and spontaneity's pen,
We'll write silly tales and start over again.

Navigating the Sea of Second-Guesses

With a map made of jelly and a ship built of cheese,
I set sail for answers, caught up in the breeze.
Each wave brings a question, a wobbly doubt,
But what if I just drift? That's fun, there's no route!

The compass spins wildly, it laughs at my fret,
As I program my mind like a catchy duet.
The sails flap like socks that don't match in the wash,
Who knew navigating could be such a nosh?

Oh, seas of the second-guess wash over me here,
It's a cartoonish dance sprinkled with cheer.
I'll hoist up my giggles and flip my regret,
And toast to the moments I won't soon forget!

So grab all your doubts and let's sail on ahead,
With laughter our anchor, we'll face what's unsaid.
The ocean is vast, but joy bubbles high,
In the sea of second-guesses, we'll laugh till we cry!

The Labyrinth of Thoughts

In the maze of my head, I roam,
Chasing answers that feel like smoke.
Round and round, I twirl with glee,
Finding meaning in a rubber chicken joke.

Does a sandwich really exist?
If no one eats it, what's the game?
I ponder fate while sipping tea,
As the toaster quietly calls my name.

Lost in theories, my mind's a whirl,
Should I question if fish wear shoes?
A cat named Whiskers may know the truth,
Or maybe it's the squirrel on the pews.

With thoughts like balloons, I float in air,
Searching for wisdom in a pie slice.
Each layer brings laughter, oh what a flair,
Perhaps I'll find peace with a roll of dice.

Whispering Shadows of Clarity

A shadow whispers, 'What's the plan?'
While I recount all my nighttime snacks.
Is life just crumbs spread through the land?
Or are we just dust with silly acts?

The moon plays tricks with twinkling eyes,
As confetti falls from trees at noon.
Do we dance with fireflies in disguise?
Or just twirl under a paper moon?

Philosophers debating the cheese,
On pizzas served at pizza pie wars.
Eureka moments come with a sneeze,
Is enlightenment found in candy stores?

So let's laugh at the questions in the dark,
Shout answers to stars that never reply.
In whispers of shadows, we leave our mark,
Perhaps life's just a joke in the sky.

The Weight of Questioning Stars

Stars giggle down from their lofty posts,
I squint and wonder if they're all drunk.
They peer at me, my cosmic hosts,
As I wear the puzzlement like a funk.

Galaxies swirl with curious designs,
Should I ask if I'm really alive?
Or contemplate whether toast can shine?
The answer escapes like a flightless dive.

Lights flicker like they're playing tag,
While my brain's doing cartwheels in despair.
Is this what grown-ups call a gag?
Or am I just on a cosmic dare?

In the weight of stars, I float and sway,
Chasing thoughts like jellybeans in the night.
If laughter's the answer, I'd say yay,
Now someone just find a cake for delight!

Riddles Amidst the Silence

Silence speaks in riddles, oh so sly,
Like tangerines hiding amongst the fries.
I laugh at questions that drift on by,
As I ponder truths in a game of lies.

Is a purple cow just an urban tale?
Or are cows skilled in the art of disguise?
With each query, my thoughts set sail,
Exploring the universe with fishy pies.

The crickets chirp their cryptic tunes,
While I scratch my head like a lost raccoon.
Are we just marionettes or cartoons?
In a world of riddles, we dance to the moon.

So here's to laughter in the quiet night,
Where questions poke fun with a tiny wink.
I'll sip my drink under starlit light,
And dance in the chaos of what I think.

The Complexity of Clarity

I ponder my breakfast choice,
Is cereal wise, or a poor voice?
Milk or yogurt, they both stare,
Decisions like these, oh, what a scare!

Why's the sky blue? Why's grass green?
Existential questions, I must glean.
Should I wear shoes, or go with flair?
Why does my toaster have two slots, I swear?

Threads of Intricate Reflection

I stared at my shoes, laced up tight,
Should I buy red or stick with white?
Every color has its own thing,
But did I really need to think?

What if my socks don't match today?
Does it mean I've lost my way?
A fashion crisis with every step,
But wait, there's more, pause for a rep!

Gazing into the Abyss of Introspection

Mirror, mirror, what's the fuss?
Is my hair a mess, or just a plus?
Do I smile back or do I grimace?
Oh, this dance, what a wild chase!

Why do I laugh when I trip?
Maybe I'm pondering a cosmic blip?
Life's so silly, let's take a chance,
And here I am, in a noodle dance!

When Certainty Slips Away

I thought I knew my favorite song,
But is it right, or did I go wrong?
Is this the chorus, or an outro plight?
Oh, the drama, am I wrong or right?

Should I march left or right today?
Do the ducks judge, or are they gay?
In this puddle, I see my fate,
But what if it's just my lunch break?

The Geometry of Worry

Circles of doubt, they spin and swirl,
Pythagoras cries, 'What a world!'
Angles of angst, they just won't quit,
Measuring thoughts, should I worry or sit?

Triangles form of my stress and fear,
Isosceles thoughts make it all unclear.
At every vertex, a question blooms,
In this math class, who needs classrooms?

Calculating dreams, pi goes on,
But in this equation, I feel so wrong.
Proofs of happiness? They twist and bend,
A graph with no end, when will it mend?

So I write down my chaos, a messy plot,
In the geometry of worry, I find a lot.
Maybe the angles reveal some cheer,
Or just silly shapes that draw me near!

Thoughts Like Leaves in the Wind

Thoughts like leaves, they dance and dive,
Blowing in circles, alive, alive!
What did I say? Oh, where did it go?
Chasing my brain, it moves too slow.

A whisper of doubt tickles my mind,
I grab at the leaves, but they're unconfined.
Falling like autumn, a colorful spree,
I laugh at the chaos that captures me.

Branches of logic, oh what a tangled mess,
Trying to organize, I feel the stress.
"Make sense of it all!" my brain seems to shout,
Yet leaves keep on swirling, there's no way out.

In the gust of confusion, I pause and grin,
Who knew pondering could feel like a win?
As I gather my leaves and send them away,
I chuckle at thoughts that refuse to stay!

The Spiral of Analysis

Round and round in my head I go,
Analyzing each moment, what a show!
The spiral tightens with each little thought,
I'm dizzy with feelings that life has brought.

"Should I wear blue? Or maybe more tan?"
Decisions like this make me feel like a man!
I ponder spaghetti or breakfast instead,
In circles of thought, I'd rather be fed.

Email to send? Or just hit delete?
This spiral's a monster, I can't find my feet.
With every decision, confusion prevails,
Like spaghetti nests leaving me with tales.

But sometimes, I giggle, and let it all go,
In this spiral of analysis, I steal the show.
For life's just a dance with a twirl and a spin,
Embracing the messy is how I begin!

Uncharted Waters of the Mind

Set sail on thoughts, the ship's gone astray,
Across uncharted waters, I drift away.
Navigating waves of what-ifs and shoulds,
Captain of nonsense, I don't know the goods.

The compass is spinning, directions unclear,
"Is that a whale or my lingering fear?"
Fish-tales of worry swim round in my head,
In these mental oceans, I'm easily led.

Drifting through currents of endless debate,
Ahoy, matey! Do I dictate my fate?
Charts and distractions are riddled with holes,
Yet here on these waters, I find my soul rolls.

So I laugh at the unknown, my quirky crew,
With my pondering ship, I'll sail on through.
For life's like a voyage, a playful surprise,
In the uncharted waters, I'll swim, I'll rise!

The Art of Spiraling Thoughts

What's the point of breakfast? I ponder,
Last night's snack was more of a blunder.
Should I toast or just go for cereal?
Finding meaning feels so ethereal.

Is my coffee cup half full or half empty?
Why is my cat always so tempty?
If life's a puzzle, I've lost a piece,
Yet here I am, searching for some peace.

What brings joy? The weather or snacks?
Translations of smiles or climbing the tracks?
With each idea, my head starts to spin,
On this carousel, where do I begin?

They say "just breathe," but I think and sigh,
What if it's raining? Or fish learn to fly?
In the circus of thoughts, I'm the star clown,
Juggling questions, but I just fall down.

The Dance of Possibilities

Shall I wear blue or is red the new trend?
Choices abound, but when will I end?
A dance of decisions, twirling around,
I step on my toes, but hey, I'm still sound.

If I speak my truth, will it cause a scene?
Or leave folks confused, caught in between?
Disco of doubts, spin me to the floor,
Are these thoughts mine, or just echoes galore?

Maybe I'll nap, or start a new quest,
The couch looks inviting, my dreams to invest.
Should I dream big, or just keep it light?
The waltz of imagining keeps me up at night.

With every step, a new path reveals,
Life likes to tease me—oh, how it feels!
Yet with each twirl, my worries will fall,
In this grand dance, I'll just laugh through it all.

Beneath the Surface of Introspection

I dive into thought like a fish in the sea,
What's lurking below is too much for me.
Glimmers of wisdom float here and there,
But I'm caught on a hook—oh, life isn't fair!

Questions like bubbles that pop with a laugh,
Is there meaning in grappling with math?
Should I count my days or just count my sheep?
In this underwater chatter, I barely can keep.

They say to think deep, to dig for the gold,
But why's my brain icy, and my heart feeling cold?
With every pearl that I search for with glee,
I realize the ocean just wants to be free.

Sipping on seaweed, my thoughts start to swirl,
If life's a big wave, shall I twirl and whirl?
Yet just like a fish, I flounder and flop,
At the surface of meaning, I can't seem to stop.

Forks in the Road of Reasoning

Left or right? The signposts are swaying,
Should I jump in the car, or just go out playing?
Decisions are tricky, like forks made of cheese,
I'll have a taste test, if you please!

What if my path leads me down to a stream?
A logical river? Or just a bad dream?
Do I follow the map or just roam free?
The directions say "fun," but I can't quite see.

Strapping on boots for a hike up a hill,
Overthinking my steps, is it wrong? Or a thrill?
With every new turn, my mind starts to spin,
Which way to the joy? I might need a pin.

In this maze of confusion, I chuckle and cheer,
For laughter is wisdom, let's make that clear.
So here's to the forks, the twists and the bends,
Embrace them with humor, my dear, life ascends.

Threads of Anxious Dreams

In a web of wonders, I spin and twirl,
Thoughts like confetti in a wild swirl.
Should I eat toast or indulge in cake?
My midnight musings make my mind ache.

With each plan I make, a new worry grows,
Like weeds in a garden, nobody knows.
Do fish ever think about life on land?
Or maybe I need a vacation, unplanned?

The cat on the fence sings a tune so bold,
While I ponder if socks should be paired or sold.
Should I call my best friend or just stay in bed?
These trivial thoughts dance 'round in my head.

As I trip through time in a mental maze,
Pondering life's meaning in so many ways.
I laugh at my chaos, so silly and spry,
Perhaps the answer is to just eat pie!

A Journey Through Endless Speculation

Buying groceries feels like a quest,
Is almond milk better than the rest?
The bread aisle's a minefield of choices galore,
While my brain debates gluten like it's the war.

Should I ask the clerk if they know my name,
Or just quickly grab my milk and feel the shame?
Each step I take, a new riddle unfolds,
What if I'm a robot, or something so bold?

The cereal box grins like it knows the secret,
While my mind's racing, how can I beat it?
Might a blue buttercup hold the key to my fate?
I'm pretty sure destiny can't wait till eight.

As I ponder over fruit, ripe for a snack,
"Banana or apple?" has me swirling back.
In the circus of choices, I drop my cart,
Maybe the answer is just to restart!

The Layers of Lurking Anxiety

Peeling back layers like an anxious onion,
What's really lurking? It feels like a pun.
Am I overthinking, or is this a game?
Like counting the leaves on a tree, so lame.

Each layer reveals new fears left unbrushed,
Like socks in the dryer, carelessly crushed.
Should I learn to tango or just binge-watching?
Suddenly, a dance party feels so fetching!

Thoughts pile up high like a tower of blocks,
One wrong move, and they tumble like socks.
I find myself laughing at the silly scholar,
Debating with pillows, "Will I ever holler?"

By nightfall I wonder if I'll break through,
Or just bake marshmallows for a warm crew.
But as I entwine in this labyrinth dance,
I grin at my mind's wild, quirky romance!

A Canvas of Chaotic Thoughts

My mind is a canvas splattered with doubt,
With colors of worry that twist and shout.
Should I paint a sunset or an abstract spree?
Maybe a portrait of a confused me!

Each brushstroke declares a possible blunder,
Like wondering if rain can cause all that thunder.
Should I put on socks? Or is barefoot best?
Pondering life feels like a wild quest.

Do clouds think of dreams as they drift on by?
While I sit pondering which cake to try.
Life's complexities float like balloons in space,
But I'm tangled in thoughts, like a shoelace race.

In the gallery of quirks, I take a stroll,
Dancing with conundrums, playing the role.
I smile at my chaos, it's truly an art,
Maybe just laughing is the best way to start!

The Search for Comfort in Confusion

In the maze of my mind, I roam,
Searching for answers, yet feeling alone.
A sock on my left, a shoe on my right,
Maybe the couch holds the secrets tonight.

Questions like popcorn, they pop and they fizz,
Each thought a riddle, oh what a biz!
I sip my cold coffee, a joke on the brew,
What was I pondering? Oh heck, who knew?

I chase after shadows, they laugh and they dart,
Trying to solve things that tear me apart.
The cat gives me looks of profound understanding,
While I'm just here, mindlessly commanding.

But perhaps all the fuss is a comedy show,
With punchlines and gags that I'll never know.
So I cap the wild theories with whimsical fun,
And dance with confusion until the day's done.

Truths Lost in Time

I found a truth tucked beneath the bed,
It whispered sweet nonsense, then fled.
Time flipped the pages, it giggled with glee,
While I scratched my head, what could it be?

A watch that is ticking, but hours feel lost,
Was there a bargain, and what's the cost?
Nostalgia slips in like a wink from a friend,
But I can't remember where this all ends.

The clock strikes a moment forever absurd,
As I spin in circles, such wisdom unheard.
Each tick is a riddle, a puzzle to tease,
Am I wise like the turtle, or foolish like bees?

So I sit in the chaos of truth's fading light,
With a pie chart of wishes, I'm feeling contrite.
Yet laughter's my compass, as I walk the line,
Between joyous confusion and moments of shine.

Vexing the Veil of Reality

Behind a curtain, reality peeks,
It trips on the rug, and then it sneaks.
I poke at the veil with a curious hairpin,
It dances in circles, like it's wearing skin.

Every wild notion takes flight like a kite,
As I try to grab thoughts that swiftly take flight.
The fish in the pond are plotting my fall,
While I tiptoe around in a polka dot shawl.

A door creaks open, but what does it show?
An echo of laughter, a hint of a glow.
Reality giggles at my wild pursuit,
As I roll on the floor in a one-man salute.

So I wade through the murk with a smile in my heart,
The absurdity blooms; it's a fine work of art.
With a jester's hat on, I join in the spree,
And dance with the weirdness, so happy and free.

Every Thought an Echo

In the caverns of thought, I hear the loud buzz,
Each echo's a memory or just silly fuzz.
I'm lost in the chorus of what-ifs and maybes,
With echoes of past that dance like two babies.

The mirror reflects what I thought I had known,
Yet laughter reveals what I've never outgrown.
Like a clown in a funhouse, I grin at the jest,
Is this a great puzzle or just mental guest?

Every whisper a giggle, each ponder a cheer,
The walls of my brain start to spin like a sphere.
And as I juggle answers that slip through the air,
I chuckle, imagining a life full of flair.

So here's to the echoes, the madness, the plays,
I celebrate thoughts in their whimsical ways.
With humor as guide, I'll embrace every whir,
In this circus of knowledge, I happily stir.

The Tides of Speculation

Waves of thought come crashing down,
Each moment lost, I start to frown.
Am I a fish, or just a guy?
Swirling doubts that never die.

Sea of questions, be my guide,
Salty tears, I'll take in stride.
Should I leap or should I float?
Caught between a dream and a boat.

Mermaids sing of truths untold,
While I'm here just feeling cold.
Shall I swim or just recline?
Life's a joke, I wish it was mine.

Under water, I make a plea,
What's the punchline? Let me see.
Paddle faster, play the fool,
Or stay lost in this endless pool.

When Silence Speaks Loudly

In the quiet, thoughts parade,
A marching band that's newly made.
Blabbering silence fills the room,
Echoes bounce like they're on Zoom.

Do I make a move or stay?
Fingers crossed it's a good day.
Pondering if I should just dance,
Or let this awkward silence prance.

Voices in my head compete,
Shouting nonsense, oh so sweet.
I ponder, ramble, plot, and plan,
While outside, all is calm and bland.

Laughter rings in vacant halls,
As I chase these ghostly calls.
What is life, a show or play?
Guess I'll just make up my own way!

Mirrors of Existential Dread

Reflecting back, what do I see?
A puzzled face that resembles me.
Is that a frown or just a grin?
Oh look, I'm back where I begin.

Mirrored doubts, a funhouse maze,
I laugh at life's absurd displays.
What's the score? Please do the math,
Am I lost, or just on a path?

Shimmering truths, all out of phase,
Dancing shadows, a glittering haze.
Is that wisdom or just a jest?
I swear this mirror knows me best.

Pondering life as I twist and turn,
In every glance, new lessons learned.
Embrace the dread, a wacky dance,
Laugh it off, or take a chance!

The Kaleidoscope of Self-Reflection

Twist the tube, what do I see?
Colors clash; could this be me?
Shattered visions swirl around,
In this chaos, truths abound.

Every turn, a brand new hue,
Do I wish for old or new?
Splinters of thought collide with glee,
Turn the lens; set my mind free.

Patterns shift and twist my brain,
Silly shapes, a jester's gain.
Is this profound or just plain fun?
Gazing deep, I come undone.

Fleeting moments dance in sight,
I chuckle at this crazy flight.
Kaleidoscope, I tip my hat,
Chaos reigns, but I'm cool with that!

Dissecting the Essence of Now

In a coffee shop, I sip and stare,
My latte art is a masterpiece rare.
Yet, present moments slip through the cracks,
As I count each drip, my thinking attacks.

A squirrel outside dances with glee,
While I ponder deeply on life's oddity.
Why do my thoughts race like a faster train?
Is the meaning lost in my caffeine brain?

Each text that pings is a riddle in code,
Should I reply, or let my thoughts explode?
Existence feels like a circus parade,
Yet I'm stuck in the tent, feeling dismayed.

I trip on my dreams, they scatter like dust,
The now feels slippery, lost in the gust.
Yet giggles emerge as I chase fleeting light,
After all, it's just a ridiculous flight.

The Color of Uncertainty

What's the hue of doubt on a Tuesday morn?
Perhaps it's neon, or maybe, well, worn.
I mix my emotions like a child with paint,
Creating a canvas of clarity faint.

Questions float like balloons in the sky,
Do they pop from pressure or just say goodbye?
I chase them around, a balloon-toting clown,
While my thoughts in confusion spin round and round.

In a world full of choices, I'm stuck in the stall,
Should I wear polka dots or go plaid after all?
Can choices reflect what I'm meant to pursue?
Or am I just painting the same old view?

A rainbow of chaos that never quite blends,
Turns laughter to colors that twist and extend.
In this wacky adventure of looking for light,
Who needs clearer visions when confusion feels right?

Sifting Through Sands of Philosophy

At the beach, my thoughts drift like grains,
Am I wise or just digging up pains?
Philosophers say, 'Know thyself' with a grin,
I'd rather build castles than sift for the win.

Each wave that crashes brings thoughts to my shore,
I ponder deep questions — what's there to explore?
Should I chase the tide or let it chase me?
While pondering life, I spill my iced tea.

A seagull squawks some profound wisdom, I swear,
It's like Aristotle had a bird's main affair.
Or maybe I just really need a snack,
Philosophy's easier with salt on my back.

In the sands, I write, then the tide rushes in,
Leaving me giggling at my existential spin.
So let's toast to confusion with a pastry or two,
Maybe the answer is frosting, who knew?

When Clarity Becomes Confusing

I had a moment, clear as glass,
Then I tripped on a thought and fell on my... pass.
Oh clarity, why do you play hide and seek?
It should be simple, not feeling so bleak.

Like a puzzle missing the edge pieces now,
I scratch my head, and my eyebrows are wow!
Do I search for answers in the fridge once more?
Or meditate deeply on what's behind that door?

I wrote a list, but then lost my pen,
Rethinking life in the fridge, where's my zen?
The answers I seek are under my hat,
Or perhaps with the cat, who just likes to chat.

So here's to confusion, my quirky old friend,
You bring me joy right up to the end.
In this circus of thoughts, we're just having fun,
Who needs clear answers when chaos has spun?

Chasing Shadows in the Mind

In the labyrinth of thought, I roam,
Chasing shadows that feel like home.
With every twist, I lose the trail,
Is it wisdom, or just a fairytale?

A pondering squirrel inside my head,
Collecting acorns of what I said.
Nonsense dances like a cheeky sprite,
Oh, the depth of my plight is quite a sight!

I wonder if life plays hide and seek,
With answers that are sure to tweak.
I laugh at questions I dare to ask,
As clarity wears an elusive mask.

When the clock ticks, it makes a sound,
In this circus of thoughts I've found.
I juggle doubts, I tumble down,
Finding joy in wearing confusion's crown.

Fractured Moments of Clarity

Once a bright bulb flickered on,
Now it hums a silly song.
In fragments, clarity's ghost does dance,
Whispering secrets of happenstance.

I take a sip of my deep thought brew,
Only to realize, it's odd and blue.
A stitch in time can still unravel,
As I ride the thought train that won't travel.

I ponder why socks go missing at night,
Or how my dreams play games in flight.
One moment wise, the next absurd,
I find humor in wisdom deferred.

So here I sit, with tea and glee,
In fractured thoughts, I can be free.
Between the laughter and the sighs,
Live moments that wear funny ties.

The Compass of Confusion

My compass spins like a roller ball,
Pointing north to a summer squall.
Each direction seems to laugh and tease,
Navigating dreams like a dandelion breeze.

I asked the stars for a guiding light,
They winked at me, "You're doing alright!"
With maps that fold into paper planes,
I fly through riddles, dodging all stains.

A sticky note with wisdom scribbled,
Is now a mirror where thoughts are whittled.
In chaos where musings often brawl,
I toss my worries and recall:

The compass spins, but what of it?
Life's a dance, where we all sit.
With giggles echoing, we'll lose the way,
But that's the fun in the wild play.

Stars in the Abyss of Thought

Gazing up at the cosmic jest,
Where stars twinkle and dreams invest.
In the vastness, questions like comets soar,
While answers tease us at the door.

Beneath the moon, I toss confessions,
Chasing thoughts like playful obsessions.
Each 'why' and 'what' flirts with my head,
As delightfully tangled as yarn on my bed.

Through the abyss, I craft my schemes,
Stitching laughter into stitched-up dreams.
Yet each revelation, just a little joke,
In the universe's big, cosmic cloak.

So let me dance with this tangled thread,
And swap my worries for a comfy bed.
For stars, they wink with a knowing grace,
In their laughter, I find my place.

Questions Like Autumn Leaves

Why does the cat stare at the wall?
Is it pondering the universe or just bored with it all?
Do ants have existential dread?
Or do they just think of crumbs and bread?

When do socks truly lose their mates?
Is it destiny or just bizarre fates?
Are chairs just sad they can't dance?
While I sit here lost in my trance?

Why do cucumbers taste like green?
And why is a pickle the prettiest bean?
Do trees gossip when we aren't around?
Or do they just moan with a creaking sound?

These thoughts swirl like leaves in the breeze,
Making my head spin with delightful unease.
While I laugh at the chaos in my brain,
And ponder if these musings are really insane.

A Journey through Infinite Whys

Why is the sky so big and blue?
Does it cry when it's cloudy too?
What makes Mondays feel like a chore?
Is it the coffee or a cosmic score?

Do fish have a way to complain?
Or are they just swimming in endless rain?
Do sandwiches dream of being hot?
Or are they content in their cold little spot?

Why do shoes always seem to hide?
Is it because they don't like this ride?
Do worms ever wish they could fly?
Or are they happy to wiggle and sigh?

Each question pops like a bubble of fun,
Leaving me giddy, wondering who won.
As I muse on all that seems askew,
I can't help but laugh at this ridiculous view.

The Unfinished Canvas of Existence

Life's a canvas with splashes of doubt,
I scribble and doodle but don't know what's out.
Is the meaning a shade called 'Minty Green'?
Or a swath of confusion, unseen?

With paintbrush in hand, I take a wack,
Creating a masterpiece, but wait—where's the snack?
Can I paint a thought without picking a hue?
Or will I just smudge it and start feeling blue?

Do clouds giggle at my jumbled art?
Or do they wonder what's wrong in my heart?
In this gallery, I'm both artist and foe,
Giggling as I stumble, chasing the glow.

With every stroke, I feel quite absurd,
Like a poet who finds their own rhymes are blurred.
Yet even in chaos, laughter will reign,
In this abstract world where I dance on my brain.

Dance of the Overwrought Mind

My thoughts are a dance, a waltz gone awry,
As I twirl with questions that pass by the sky.
Do clouds even care if I ponder their shape?
Or are they too busy making raindrop escape?

Each thought is a pirouette on a dime,
While I juggle reasons like a clown out of time.
Is the moon just a nightlight for creatures unseen?
Or a narcissist shining, caught in a sheen?

My brain throws a party, the dance floor's all set,
With the DJ just playing my own silly fret.
Is laughter the ribbon that ties it all true?
Or is it the confetti that keeps me askew?

As I'm lost in this fiesta of whimsical fears,
I giggle at life and all its strange gears.
While I dance with my thoughts through the comedic grind,
I find joy in the chaos—oh, what a fun bind!

The Parable of Pondering

In a land where thoughts collide,
A squirrel questioned what's inside.
He pondered nuts beneath the trees,
Wondering why he can't find peace.

A butterfly flits with grand designs,
Asks the sun about the signs.
"Are we more than colors?" it frets,
While chasing shadows and regrets.

An ant has doubts about the hill,
Is there a purpose in the drill?
He lifts a crumb with serious grace,
As if decoding life's big race.

The jokes of life are never clear,
Each question draws a chuckling cheer.
So sit back, enjoy the show,
And let the ponderings just flow.

Layers of Uncertainty

A pickle jar with thoughts so thick,
Trying to grasp what makes us tick.
Each layer peeled reveals more gloom,
Yet here I am, in full costume.

A fish once thought it knew the sea,
But wonders if it's really free.
Does the ocean dream of skies?
Or is it just fishy lies?

An onion's cries are heard at night,
As layers shed in pure fright.
"Am I just food or more profound?"
Yet on the plate, it turns around.

So let's unwrap the silly stuff,
And laugh through layers, light and tough.
In every doubt, there hides a grin,
Like a playful dance that won't give in.

The Infinite Loop of Inquiry

In circles we dance, a merry-go-round,
A question pops up, our thoughts unbound.
Why is the sky so vast and blue?
Yet my head hits the ceiling too.

Like a cat chasing its own tail,
We ask if life's a grand fairy tale.
Is the grass greener on the other side?
Or just a trick to turn the tide?

A parrot squawks, 'What's life's big plan?'
Mimicking questions, soon it ran.
It's caught in loops, and we all laugh,
A sketchy map to find the path.

So spin around and take a leap,
Grab the giggles, let worries sleep.
The infinite query leads to fun,
And that's the point when day is done.

Buried Beneath the Surface

They dug a hole to find the truth,
Uncovered dirt, but lost their youth.
A shovel full of what's real fun,
The deeper they went, the more they spun.

A mole chewed thoughts, all wrinkled eyes,
He said, "Dig deeper; it's no surprise!"
Each answer pulled was covered in grime,
And still they searched, in endless time.

A treasure chest of silly trends,
Full of wonders, yet no amends.
Inside were socks and books askew,
The meaning rests far out of view.

So let's embrace the burly mess,
And dig with joy, not just to impress.
For under the surface, where laughter lies,
We find the quirky truth in disguise.